the guide to owning a
Cat

M000312909

Donald Vaughan

T.F.H. Publications, Inc.
One TFH Plaza
Third and Union Avenues
Neptune City, NJ 07753

ISBN 0-7938-2174-6

Printed and Distributed by T.F.H. Publications, Inc.
Neptune City, NJ

Contents

The History of Domestic Cats 3

Selecting a Cat or Kitten 8

Preparing for Your New Cat .24

Behavior and Training 38

Your Cat's Health 50

Index 64

The History of Domestic Cats

Cats have been a companion to humans for thousands of years, although it's difficult to say who first adopted whom. Genetic information suggests that the varied housecats we know today are almost all descended from African wild cats. The ancient Egyptians, many of whom worshiped cats as sacred animals, first actively domesticated them. However, evidence indicates that cats began associating with man long before that. Most experts believe that cats were some of the

Cats chose to live close to humans long before they were fully domesticated. Early cats scavenged for food in human trash and hunted in granaries.

Wild (feral) cats have been able to thrive in places that humans have long since abandoned, demonstrating their adaptability.

very first animals to live close to humans intentionally, scavenging food at campsites and hunting for vermin around granaries as far back as 8000 BC, when the first nomadic tribes settled into communal life.

The earliest wild cats to consort with man almost certainly were fearful of them, as any wild animal is, and probably did not actually share living quarters with humans for several generations. But it can be assumed that both cat and human quickly realized the mutual benefits of cohabitation (food and shelter for the cat, companionship for humans), and that later generations of felines lived willingly with their two-legged "masters," a phenomenon known as "self-domestication." This process is decidedly different from the domestication of wild dogs, which were pack animals (as contemporary dogs are)

and lived most successfully and happily in groups. Cats, as we all know, are far more solitary in temperament, so the earliest species had little innate need to live in families. They did so only because it made their lives easier with regard to food and shelter.

Once cats became domesticated, their range expanded along with that of humans. The appearance of local domestic cat populations correlates perfectly with the spread of civilization from the Middle East, and domestic cats can now be found on every continent except Antarctica and most of the oceanic islands. Cats, as most owners know, are very adaptable, and sustained populations of wild (feral) cats can be found in areas where they were not originally introduced. In addition, thriving

Many of today's cat breeds look quite a bit like the African wild cats from which they descended.

populations of cats also inhabit areas that have long been abandoned by humans.

The African wild cats from which most of today's pets are descended look very much like contemporary tabbies, although the wild cats are a little larger in size. There are, however, some distinct differences, with the most intriguing being that domestic cats have longer intestines. This is probably because cats have gone from being predators to scavengers over the years, so their diets are now lower in protein. According to veterinary experts, a longer intestinal tract helps to maximize the absorption of amino acids from a lower-protein diet.

Like their ancestors, today's cats are hunter-scavengers, with an emphasis on scavenging. Today's housecats don't need to hunt, and their predatory instincts have become somewhat dulled as a result. This is true even of feral cats that must fend for themselves. A study of the stomach contents of stray city cats found that only three percent of their diet consisted of prey such as birds and rodents. The rest was refuse scavenged from garbage cans and trash dumps.

ONE BIG FAMILY

All cats are related, regardless of size. Whether lion or tiger, tabby or Siamese, they all belong to the cat family Felidae, in the order Carnivora. There are 36 different species of cat in the wild, ranging from the well known, such as the lion, to small, odd breeds that most people never see, such as the jaguarundi.

Centuries of breeding have resulted in dozens of distinct and unique-looking

There are 36 different species of cat in the wild. Big or small, all cats are members of the same scientific family.

Each cat has a unique personality and temperament, and there is a perfect cat out there for everyone. Take your time before making your selection.

domestic cats. Unlike dogs, which have been bred for specific tasks such as hunting and guarding, cats have been bred primarily for their beauty and personality. Aside from minor differences in coat length, color, and body shape, the domestic cat of today looks quite a bit like its earliest ancestors. Indeed, the characteristics shared by cats large and small are intriguing. They include the following:

- Male and female cats look similar (with the exception of lions, in which the male has a noticeable mane while the female does not).
- All cats walk on their toes, with their steps made silent by cushioned pads. This helps them sneak up on their prey unnoticed and move quickly when they have to pounce. One cat, the cheetah, is fast enough to chase down its prey. Cheetahs have been clocked at 70 miles per hour in short sprints.
- All cats have an exceptional sense of balance, which enables them to leap and pounce on their prey with amazing accuracy.
- All cats have extremely sensitive sight and hearing.
- Most cats are solitary animals. The best-known exception is the lion, which prefers to hunt in groups known as "prides."

In the eyes of many non-cat owners, a cat is a cat is a cat. However, this sentiment is not only wrong but grossly unfair. As anyone who has owned more than one cat will tell you, cats are as different in personality and temperament as human beings. Some like to play and explore all the time, while others prefer simply to snooze the day away. Some love to be in the company of people, while others are a little bit shy. Such differences in personality and temperament are a good thing, because it means that regardless of your taste and requirements, there is almost certainly a cat out there for you. All you have to do is find her.

Selecting a Cat or Kitten

Selecting a cat is not a decision that should be made lightly. You're bringing another living creature into your life, and there are a lot of factors to consider for both you and your new pet.

One of the first questions you should ask yourself is whether you want a kitten

Remember that your cat will live with you for many years. Carefully consider all of your options before making your final choice.

or a grown cat. Many people are drawn to kittens because they are so cute and cuddly, but mature cats offer a lot of advantages, too. To help you make the right decision, consider the following:

Who will take care of your new pet? Kittens are more fragile than older cats, and young children may inadvertently hurt them during rough play. If the pet is for a small child, an easygoing older cat may be a wiser choice. This is also true if the cat will be living with someone who is older or in poor health—kittens are rambunctious animals that may be more than an older person can safely handle.

How much time will you be able to devote to training your new kitty? Kittens require a lot of supervision, and it will be your job to make sure your pet knows how to use the litter box, play safely, and not shred your expensive new sofa with her tiny—but very sharp—claws. If you are looking for companionship but don't have a lot of extra time to train your cat, an older animal may be better for you.

Where will your new cat be living? Kittens, like small children, always seem to get into places where they don't belong. They are naturally curious and love to explore, which can present problems if your house is large, full of hidden spaces, or difficult to "kitten-proof." Again, an older cat with a slower temperament may be a better pet in a situation like this.

That's not to say, of course, that kittens don't make wonderful pets. They do—under the right circumstances. Indeed, kittens are great for older children aged seven years and up as well as for adults with lots of energy. They are cute and provide their owners with plenty of exercise. Watching kittens grow up can be an enriching life experience, so if you think a kitten will fit well into your lifestyle, go for it!

Kittens are fragile, and young children may inadvertently hurt them during rough play. An older cat may be a better choice for households with young children.

AT WHAT AGE?

How old should a kitten be before she can safely be adopted? That's an important question, because a kitten that is taken from her mother before she is properly

Make sure to "kitten-proof" your house before bringing a kitten home, or you may find her getting into places where she doesn't belong.

weaned may suffer from health and socialization problems.

A reputable breeder will not adopt out a kitten before the kitten is between 14 and 16 weeks of age. At this age, most kittens are sufficiently weaned off of their mother's milk, a diet that has helped to strengthen their young immune systems, and properly socialized, which will help the kittens adapt to their new family and surroundings. The very youngest age at which a kitten should be adopted is ten weeks, by which time she has probably developed most of the skills and abilities she will need as an adult. But the longer she can spend with her mother and littermates, the better.

If possible, select a kitten that has been around people—both children and

Kittens should stay with their mother until they are fully weaned, usually between 14 and 16 weeks old.

adults—during her formative months. Interaction with humans as well as other cats will make for a well-rounded pet that gets along well with just about everyone. A kitten that has not been properly socialized may exhibit serious behavior problems, including fearfulness and anxiety, which often manifests in angry biting, scratching, hissing, and other difficulties. These problems can be corrected, but that will take a lot of time and effort.

PUREBRED OR MIXED BREED?

Once you've decided whether to get a kitten or a grown cat, it's time to determine what kind. Some people don't care—the first cat they fall in love with is the one they bring home, regardless of breed. Others are more particular, preferring a specific breed or characteristic, such as short hair. The choice is yours, and there is no right or wrong.

For older children and adults with lots of energy, kittens make wonderful pets. They are adorable and very entertaining.

The majority of cats in the US are mixed breed, meaning their genetic makeup comprises two or more breeds. Mixed-breed cats may have the coloring and other characteristics of the dominant breed (the exotic appearance and vocalization of a Siamese, for example), but many are simply short-haired or long-haired, with few distinguishing features. In determining whether to go with a mixed breed or a purebred animal, consider the following:

Price

Purebred cats can be expensive, especially when you buy from a pet store or a breeder who specializes in show animals. Depending on breed and other factors, a purebred cat may cost an exorbitant amount, whereas a healthy and personable mixed-breed cat may usually be adopted for considerably less at your local animal shelter. However, don't discount shelters if you're looking for a purebred pet. Very often, purebred cats are abandoned for one reason or another, and they don't cost any more to adopt than a mixed breed. So if you have your heart set on a Himalayan, for example, and you're not in a particular hurry, it may be worth your while to visit your local animal shelters on a weekly basis until one shows up. Many shelters will also keep your request on file and notify you when the right animal becomes available for adoption, so don't forget to ask if this service is available.

Required Care

Many purebred cats require a lot of maintenance, especially long-haired breeds such as Persians and Himalayans. They must be groomed on a regular basis (sometimes daily) to avoid mats in their fur and other problems such as mucous buildup around their eyes.

Temperament

Some purebred cats, such as Burmese, Siamese, and Orientals, can be extremely demanding. They are naturally curious animals that enjoy playing and exploring, and they don't like to be left alone for extended periods. They can also be very vocal, which some people may find irritating.

Of course, many of these considerations also apply to mixed-breed cats. For example, a long-haired mixed breed must receive the same amount of grooming and care as a long-haired purebred. When it comes times to make your final decision, listen to your heart as well as your brain. Most people find personality to be more important than pedigree.

Himalayan cat

MOST POPULAR PUREBREDS

The following is a quick review of the ten most popular breeds of cat in the US, as determined by the Cat Fanciers' Association:

Persian. A long-haired cat, bred in a variety of colors. Known for its friendly, affectionate, laid-back temperament. Requires a lot of grooming.

Maine Coon. One of the largest breeds of cat, intelligent and sweet-natured. Also a long-haired breed, it requires frequent grooming.

Siamese. An extremely intelligent breed that comes in a wide variety of colorings. Very talkative and personable, with a very high activity level. Requires very little grooming.

Exotic Shorthair. A combination of the American Shorthair and the Persian, this is an extremely cute breed with a short, snub nose and wide-set ears. Friendly and affectionate. Despite its name, it requires quite a bit of grooming.

Abyssinian. In turn affectionate and independent, this active short-haired breed is usually a red ("ruddy") color with ticked fur. Abys are very intelligent, elegant cats with a wild, ancient Egyptian appearance.

Scottish Fold. Sweet-natured, gentle, and friendly in temperament, this breed is distinguished by its unique folded ears and large round eyes. Has a thick, dense coat and requires regular grooming.

Oriental Shorthair. Friendly and inquisitive, this breed, which is an offshoot of the Siamese breed that comes in dozens of colors, is quite intelligent and enjoys company. Requires occasional grooming.

American Shorthair. Outgoing, affectionate, and quite intelligent in temperament, this muscular cat has been bred in a number of unique colorings. Its coat is short and thick and requires regular grooming.

Birman. Known for its gorgeous colorings, this long-haired breed is intelligent, friendly, and talkative. Due to the length and density of its coat, it requires frequent grooming.

Tonkinese. Somewhat similar to the Siamese in appearance, this short-haired breed is inquisitive, intelligent, active, and outgoing. Can be talkative, but is quieter than the Siamese. Requires little grooming.

FINDING YOUR CAT

One thing is for certain: There is no shortage of available cats! Cats in need of good homes can be found in the classified ads of your local newspaper, on notices in supermarkets, from breeders, from pet stores, and even from friends and neighbors. Sadly, there are so many unwanted cats that millions are destroyed each year for lack of homes.

Once you've decided what kind of cat you want and what age, the fun really starts—finding the right pet for you. It can be a challenging endeavor, but the results will be well worth your efforts.

Shelter Cats

Where to begin? Unless you specifically want a purebred cat or a breed that's less common, the best place to start your search is your local animal shelter. Most communities have several animal facilities, both public and private, and all will have a wide selection of homeless kitties from which to choose. In fact, you may be so overwhelmed by the number of cats vying for your attention that you find it impossible to make a choice. But adopting a cat is like buying a car—you shouldn't take the first one that catches your eye. In fact, you should do a lot of shopping around before making your final decision. Visit all of the shelters in your area to see what they have available. If possible, play with some of the animals that fit your criteria to see how they react to you. Take notes, then weigh the pros and cons of the cats that have made the top of your list.

There are many places to search for the perfect cat. Your local animal shelter is a great place to start.

This may sound time-consuming, but it's the best way for you to make such an important life decision. There are a lot of factors to consider when acquiring a cat, and your decision shouldn't be made in haste or forced on you by other family members. When you do make your final choice, it will be the right one. The only downside to shopping around is that the cat at the top of your list may be adopted out before you return for her. But don't worry, there will be many others begging you to take them home!

Adoption policies vary from shelter to shelter and municipality to municipality, but in general, the stricter the requirements, the better the facility because it shows they really care about the animals in their custody. Depending on the shelter, you may be required to fill out a lengthy adoption form, detail your past pet experiences, and even provide veterinary and character references. Many shelters also require you to have your new cat spayed or neutered before you can take her home, and most include the cost of this procedure in the adoption price. They also may require that you have the cat properly identified with a tattoo or microchip in case she gets lost.

A word of warning: Be wary of shelter cats that don't appear to be in the best of health. Shelters are not very pleasant places for cats, and it's common for a cat to show signs of stress while caged. But avoid obvious signs of ill health, such as a discharge from the eyes or nose, sneezes, coughs, or other signs of a respiratory

Visit several breeders before purchasing your cat. Check to see that the cats are living in a clean, healthy environment.

knowledgeable about the breed she raises and will sell you a healthy, well-adjusted cat. The key word here is "reputable." Just because someone advertises herself as a cat breeder doesn't mean she is an authority or that the animals she sells are properly bred and in good health.

How can you tell if a local breeder is someone that you should deal with? Ask around. What is the breeder's reputation among local veterinarians, cat club officials, and cat owners? Is she known for selling healthy animals? Are previous customers satisfied? (Ask the breeder for references, and walk away if she refuses.) A negative comment from any of these sources doesn't necessarily mean that a breeder isn't professional or doesn't sell quality animals, but it should give you pause to think.

After you've checked references, visit the breeder and tour her home or facility. Watch for signs of neglect or that the operation is actually a "kitten mill," evidenced by large numbers of cats confined to small quarters or living in filth. Are all of the cats healthy, energetic, and well socialized? Have they been around people and do they enjoy human company? Are they being offered after they're fully weaned? Does the breeder ask as many questions about you as you do about her? The answer to all of these questions should be yes.

Many breeders never sell to the general public but only to other breeders, because their intent is not to provide pets but to maintain and improve their specific

disorder, fur missing in patches or other indications of a parasitic infection, open sores, or an emaciated appearance. Reputable shelters provide good veterinary care to all of their animals and separate those that are obviously ill, but some shelters are more lax about this than others. If you have a bad feeling about a particular facility, leave and go somewhere else.

Breeders

Professional cat breeders are a good option when looking for a specific breed of cat, such as a Siamese, Persian, or Himalayan. A reputable breeder is very breed. This is especially true of those who specialize in rare breeds. However, many breeders also show their cats and are willing to sell those that are less-than-perfect show specimens—but still wonderful in every other way—to good homes. The price charged by a breeder may be considerably more than you would pay at a local shelter, but it should be comparable to or less than the prices charged by a commercial pet store.

One final note: When buying from a breeder, ask if she offers a guarantee regarding your cat's health. A reputable breeder will refund your money if a veterinarian finds a serious health problem in your new kitty within a reasonable period of time. A breeder who says "all sales final" should be viewed with caution.

Veterinarians, Friends, and Neighbors

We've all seen notices for free kittens in our veterinarian's office or on the bulletin board at church or our local grocery store. Should you consider such a source for your new pet? The answer is yes—and no. You can't beat the price, but free animals should be considered with caution, because very often you don't know what you're getting until it's too late.

By taking a kitten from a friend, neighbor, or stranger, you're providing a home to a cat that might otherwise end up in an animal-control shelter or simply abandoned on the roadside. That's a very

A "free" kitten could turn out to be very expensive if she isn't healthy. Make sure to have the cat thoroughly checked by your vet before taking her home.

A free adult cat will probably be fixed, well socialized, and vaccinated. However, she may have a hidden behavior problem, so make sure to ask plenty of questions before taking your new pet home.

philanthropic gesture, and there's a special place in heaven for people who do that. But at the same time, free kittens very often come from unneutered cats that roam free outdoors, and that's not good. You don't know what the lineage is, you're encouraging irresponsible pet ownership, and worse, free-range cats are exposed to a wide range of diseases and medical conditions that can also manifest themselves in your new kitten, such as parasites. If you do adopt a free kitten—especially from someone you don't know—take her to a veterinarian immediately for a full checkup. And remember, if your veterinarian finds something wrong with your new kitten, it's your responsibility. Most free pets are nonreturnable.

The situation is slightly different with adult cats. Adult cats become available for a wide range of legitimate reasons—the owner can no longer take care of the cat, someone in the family has developed an allergy, or the owners are moving and can't take the cat with them. It's not the cat's fault, nor have the owners necessarily been irresponsible; circumstances have merely changed.

Acquiring an adult cat from friends, neighbors, or strangers isn't quite as risky as adopting a kitten, but you should still be careful. On the plus side, an adult cat will probably be fixed, well socialized, and at ease around people. She should have received all of her vaccinations and be in good health. In other words, she's a terrific pet that is simply in need of someone to care for her.

On the downside, an adult cat may have a behavior problem that you won't find out about until it's too late, such as urinating or defecating outside her litter box, scratching furniture, or meowing incessantly. All of these can be corrected, but do you really need the aggravation?

You're usually safe accepting an adult cat from a friend or acquaintance. In fact, if the owner is a good friend, you and the cat are probably already pals. But before accepting an adult cat from a stranger, ask some questions. Why is it necessary for the person to get rid of the cat? Has she had all of her vaccinations? (If the answer is yes, ask for proof.) Does she have any known health or behavior problems? (The person may not be entirely truthful, so look for signs of bad behavior, such as clawed furniture, stains on the carpet, or a pervasive urine smell). Is she friendly around strangers? To test this last one, ask to spend a few minutes alone with the animal. Does she come to you willingly and readily? Is she playful, or does she exhibit fear and anxiety? A cat that hisses and lashes out at strangers is not well socialized and should be avoided.

As with a new kitten, a newly adopted adult cat should be taken to a veterinarian right away for a complete examination. Even if the previous owner swears to her good health, it's better to be safe than sorry. In addition, an examination will give you a baseline for comparison at all future veterinary visits.

Pet Stores

It's the rare pet store that doesn't have at least some cats for sale. They're usually frolicking kittens, so adorable that it's difficult to resist them. That's just what the store is counting on! But are pet stores really a good place to buy a new cat? That depends.

Some of the cats "sold" in pet stores today are actually shelter cats. Many of the larger chain stores (and lots of small stores, too) work with local shelters to provide greater exposure to potential homes for shelter animals. If this is the case in your pet store, refer to the "shelter cats" section of this book for advice on adopting one of these pets.

However, some pet stores do sell purebred cats and kittens. Reputable pet stores acquire their purebred feline stock from reputable breeders, who sell only healthy, well-adjusted animals. But not all pet stores are reputable. Many acquire cats from so-called "kitten mills," people who breed cats wholesale with the sole intent of selling them to pet stores for an easy profit. Their breeding stock often spend their entire lives in squalid, inhumane conditions, and when they are old or unable to bear kittens anymore, they are disposed of as quickly as yesterday's garbage. It's an ugly profession that, sadly, is difficult to eliminate, simply because most state animal-control agencies are so short-staffed.

If you do decide to buy a cat from a pet store, ask for written proof of the animal's background. Where did the store acquire the cat? What assurances do you have that the cat did not come from a kitten mill? As with breeders, check out the reputation of the pet store with local veterinarians and animal control officials. Most importantly, make sure that the cat

Cats often find their owners instead of the other way round. If a lovable stray adopts you, it might be the beginning of a wonderful, lifelong friendship.

20

THE GUIDE TO OWNING A CAT

comes with a money-back guarantee in case your veterinarian detects a serious health problem. Stores that refuse to take back unhealthy cats should be avoided.

When a Cat Finds You

Very often, cats enter our lives when we least expect it. A stray finds her way to your doorstep, and before you know it, you've been adopted. I know a lot of people who have acquired cats in this manner, and most of their stories have happy endings. But as with anything unknown, you should exercise caution and good judgement before bringing a stray or feral cat into your life.

The very first thing you should do when a cat finds you is make sure she hasn't simply wandered away from someone else. A people-friendly personality is an indicator that the cat has been around humans a lot and may be someone else's pet that is merely out for a stroll. Before adopting such an animal yourself, do all you can to make sure she's really available. Examine the animal for identification, such as a collar tag, a tattoo on her ear or the inside of her leg, or a microchip just under the skin on the back of her neck or near her shoulder blades. (Such chips are about the size of a grain of rice, but they can be detected by gently kneading the skin in these areas.) In addition, you should scan the classified ads for lost cats and place a "found cat" ad yourself, offering a general description of the animal and where you found it. Leave out an important detail, such as a ring on the tail or dark coloration on one foot, so that the true owner will be able to identify the cat. You should also check notices on local bulletin boards, call area animal control facilities, and let your neighbors know that you have found a stray cat.

If no one comes forward, the cat is yours to keep. Once you've decided to bring the cat into your family, the first thing you should do is take her to a veterinarian for a complete checkup. This is vitally important, because an outdoor cat can acquire a wide range of diseases, from rabies to feline leukemia to FIV, and your new pet can quickly spread these diseases to other cats (and, with certain diseases, people) in your family. A visit to the vet is important, too, because your new pet should immediately be vaccinated for rabies and other disorders (requirements vary from region to region). Your new pet may already have received her shots, but you can't know for sure. It's always wise to err on the side of caution.

If you're lucky, your new cat will behave impeccably, using her litter box and sharpening her claws on a scratching post rather than on your favorite furniture. But cats that have spent a lot of time on their own outdoors often develop bad habits that are difficult to break. They may also demonstrate aggressive behavior against other animals and people in your house. Keep this in mind when deciding whether to adopt a stray. Bad behavior can be corrected, but it takes time and patience. The question you must ask yourself is: Is this animal worth it?

Many pet owners find that two cats are easier to care for then one, because they keep each other company.

ONE CAT, TWO CATS...HOW MANY IS ENOUGH?

The number of cats that's right for you is a determination only you can make. Most people find that two cats are ideal because the cats can keep each other company while their owners are away. However, unlike dogs, which are pack animals by nature and thus do better in groups, cats are typically solitary creatures, so it's not absolutely necessary to provide them with feline companionship. Most cats do well by themselves and spend their time sleeping, playing, or exploring when their owners are out of the house.

The number of cats that you keep as pets should be limited to the number you can easily and properly care for. We've all seen news articles about people who have been found with dozens of cats in their homes, and it's seldom a pleasant situation for anyone. Luckily, cases like this are rare, and they are usually a sign of an eccentric personality.

It's not uncommon, however, for cat lovers to keep three, four, and even five or more cats in their homes successfully. If you have the space and the money to do this, and the animals in your care are healthy and get along well, that's fine. But if you find yourself spending less on essential items for your family so that you can buy cat food or litter, it may be time to dramatically reduce the number of pets in your home.

There are several important factors to consider when determining the number of cats that's best for you.

Space

If you live in an apartment or small house, two cats is probably the most you should adopt. If your home is considerably larger, then you can add a couple more if you so desire. Lots of cats in small quarters can result in an unpleasant smell no matter how often you change the litter, and you also run the risk of having to cope with destructive or aggressive behavior because your pets have no place to roam or to call their own.

Cost

Keeping cats isn't cheap. You must provide food, litter, toys, and routine veterinary care for every animal in your charge. Every cat you acquire increases this required expense proportionally.

Time and Energy

Cats aren't something you can bring home and then largely ignore, like a goldfish. They are intelligent creatures that make demands on your time and energy, and the more cats you have, the more time you must spend with them. If you live a hectic lifestyle, adopting five cats is probably a bad idea because you simply won't be able to spend adequate time with them all. In such cases, one or two cats is much more reasonable.

Rules and Regulations

Some apartment complexes and housing developments limit the number of pets you

Some cats are much happier as solitary pets. It's important to respect the unique needs and personality of your beloved kitty.

can own. It's always a good idea to check into this before you acquire a menagerie.

Personality

Like people, some cats are gregarious and friendly, while others are more solitary. Before bringing multiple animals into your home, make sure they are all well socialized and enjoy the company of other cats, or you could be asking for trouble. In our own household, our cat Rhianna let us know early on that she was the queen of the house and was unwilling to share that position with any other animal. As a result, we are a one-cat family.

Preparing for Your New Cat

Bringing your new kitty home for the first time is an exciting experience. Many cat owners say it's almost as exciting as bringing home a new baby and that you need just as many supplies!

That's an exaggeration, but not much of one. Cats, like babies, have certain needs and requirements that we, as their "parents," are obliged to satisfy. These include food and water, a litter box, toys, and so forth. It's a good idea to have all of these set up and ready before you bring your cat home for the very first time. That way, you can spend your time getting acquainted rather than racing around doing last-minute shopping.

Where should you shop for cat supplies? It doesn't really matter. Some people enjoy the convenience of a large pet-supply retail chain, while others prefer the personal service of a neighborhood mom-and-pop pet shop. Some cat owners patronize both, perhaps buying food and litter in bulk at a large retail outlet and purchasing special items, such as one-of-a-kind toys and monogrammed food bowls, from an independent retailer. Both types of stores have their advantages and disadvantages, and the final decision is up to you.

BASIC SUPPLIES

There are certain things cats must have, and certain things that could be considered luxuries. The must-haves include the following items.

Food

There are a lot of different cat foods from which to choose these days, with more being introduced all the time. The brand of food you choose is a matter of personal preference, because all national name brands meet government regulations regarding a complete and well-balanced diet. However, the same can't be said of all off-brand or regional pet foods, and these should be viewed with caution. To ensure that the food you're feeding your cat is complete and balanced, look for a statement on the label that says the food meets the nutritional guidelines established by the American Association of Feed Control Officials (AAFCO) or the equivalent organization in your country. Many companies offer special foods for the various life phases that cats go through, from kitten to old age, on the theory that a cat's nutritional requirements change as she ages. If your cat is very young, very old, or has a chronic disease, your veterinarian may recommend a special diet. Otherwise, foods labeled "feline maintenance" are usually sufficient.

Cat food comes in three forms: wet (canned), semi-moist (packets), and dry (most often packaged in boxes or bags).

Owners often fret over which food is best, but again, it boils down to personal preference because most foods are quite similar in nutritional content. Canned foods are very flavorful, but they spoil quickly if they are left out. Semi-moist foods are somewhat less flavorful, but more convenient and less prone to spoilage. Most dry foods may be left out all day without going bad, and they also offer another benefit in that dry food helps keep a cat's teeth clean. Ultimately, it all boils down to which foods your cat enjoys, how much you want to spend (canned foods tend to be a little more expensive than semi-moist or dry foods), and what's most convenient for you.

Should you feed your cat table scraps? Most veterinary nutritionists say it's okay as long as you don't overdo it. Table scraps

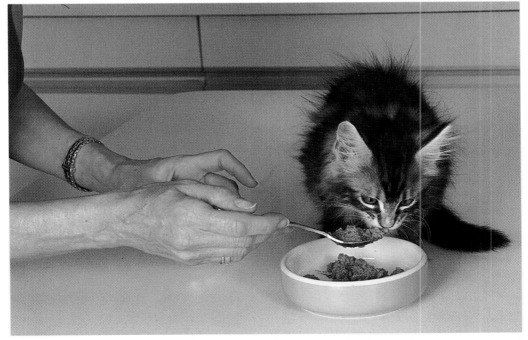

Many different types of cat food are available. Choose one that is nutritionally complete and balanced for your cat's needs.

Dry cat food is a staple of most cats' diets because it can be left out all day without going bad.

should amount to no more than ten percent of your cat's daily diet because they are not nutritionally complete and balanced. If you do feed your cat the occasional scrap of meat, make sure that you place the food in her bowl rather than feeding her from the table. Table-feeding can lead to unwanted behavior, such as begging or food-snatching.

Many cat owners worry that their cats aren't getting all the nutrients they need, even on a name-brand diet, so they add nutritional supplements to their pets' food. However, most veterinary nutritionists agree that this isn't necessary. A cat that is extremely old or afflicted with a chronic disease may need nutritional supplements, but these should be given only on the recommendation of your veterinarian.

Now that you've decided what to feed your cat, the next question is where. The location of your cat's food and water bowls should make feeding convenient for you but allow your pet some degree of privacy as she eats. You also need to make sure that your cat's food is out of the reach of small children (who, for some reason, seem to find cat food extremely tasty) and other pets, such as hungry dogs. Good locations include a laundry room, a quiet kitchen corner, or a relatively unused guest bathroom.

If you have a choice, use ceramic or metal bowls for your cat's food and water. For some reason, plastic bowls sometimes cause unsightly "feline acne," an inflamed area on a cat's chin that results from rubbing on plastic surfaces. This condition doesn't afflict all cats, but it's something to think about.

How many food bowls do you need for a multi-cat household? That really depends on the cats themselves. Cats that grew up together and are comfortable around each other probably won't mind sharing a single bowl, but if your pets are territorial or hiss in each other's presence, it's a good idea to have a bowl for each.

Litter Box

A litter box is second in importance only to food in your cat's life. Both the type of box and the type of litter you select will go a long way toward keeping both you and your pet happy, but do understand that you may have to engage in some trial and error before you get it right. Cats can be very finicky animals, and they often have their own litter box preferences. Luckily, there are a lot of choices.

The selection of boxes ranges from disposable cardboard litter boxes to sturdy plastic pans that can last a lifetime. There are even mechanical litter boxes that actually clean themselves, though satisfaction with these devices varies widely. Your best bet is a sturdy plastic pan with or without a top. Plastic cleans easily, is safe for your pet, and lasts indefinitely. It's also relatively inexpensive. A top may help keep odors contained, but if you clean your cat's box on a daily basis, a top is probably unnecessary. Even if you do get a plastic litter box, it's also a good idea to get one or two disposable pans, just in case. They come in handy if you have to travel with

Your cat prefers a clean bathroom, just as you do. Keeping her litter box clean will make for one happy kitty.

your pet or if you're litter-training kittens. They cost only a couple of dollars, and you can store them in a closet until they're needed.

As with your pet's food and water, you should keep the litter box in an area where it won't be obtrusive and where your pet can have some privacy when nature calls. An unused bathroom, pantry, laundry room, or garage are all good locations. It's okay to keep your cat's litter box in the same room as her food and water, but don't put them too close together. Cats are obsessively clean, and most of them don't like to eat too near where they relieve themselves.

What kind of litter should you use? It used to be that you didn't have much of a choice—kitty litter was kitty litter. But today, you have a wide range of litters from which to choose, including traditional clay litter, clumping litter, and even scented litter! Most cat owners find clumping litter (which hardens into an easy-to-remove ball after your cat urinates or defecates) to be the most convenient, because you don't have to change the entire litter box. You simply remove the hardened clumps every day and add a little more litter when necessary. Clumping litter costs a little more than traditional litter, but most cat owners find it to be well worth the few extra pennies. The only downside is that cats with furry paws may get clumping litter, which is very fine, between their toes and track it around the house. This problem can be eliminated by placing an

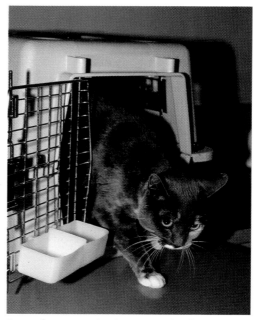

A sturdy cat carrier is a necessity for any cat-owning household. You'll need it for trips to the vet, vacations, and emergencies.

old towel beneath the litter box for your cat to wipe her paws on after she's done. Another consideration is that many clumping litters cannot be flushed down the toilet. The clumps must be placed in a plastic bag and disposed of in the garbage.

Over the past few years, a number of alternative filler materials have been introduced to the pet market. Touted as more ecologically sound than traditional clay litter, they include recycled newspaper, corncob, pine shavings, absorbent balls made from silica dioxide, and even recycled peanut shells. Some cats dislike the texture of these new materials and refuse to use them, but others manage quite well. The only way to find out is to try them on your own cat. Box filler made of recycled newspaper or other coarse materials works very well with cats that are recovering from surgery and cannot use traditional clay litter. It's absorbent, sanitary, doesn't stick to bandages or stitches, and makes cleanup a snap.

Cat Carrier

You may have been given a cardboard cat carrier when you brought your new pet home for the first time. If so, throw it away. Cardboard carriers are satisfactory for short trips, but they are too flimsy for long trips or medical emergencies. You need something far more sturdy— preferably a carrier made out of hard plastic or wood.

You may be thinking: "Why do I need a carrier? My cat will never leave the house." While it may be true that your cat will spend the vast majority of her life within the confines of your home, there will be times when you will have to take her out, such as for veterinary visits, vacations, or emergencies, and a sturdy carrier is the easiest and safest way to do that. This is especially true if you are transporting a panicked animal.

A broad selection of cat carriers, from the very cheap to the very expensive, can be found at most pet stores. A plastic carrier with small vents and a strong metal door is your best bet, because it protects both you and your kitty and is nearly impossible to escape from. Best of all, an enclosed carrier will ease your cat's anxiety because it protects her from exposure to the elements, which is the biggest problem with carriers made of mesh, wire, wicker, and similar materials.

A well-made carrier may come with a significant price tag. It may seem like a lot of money, but it's money well spent.

OPTIONAL SUPPLIES

Food, water, a litter box, and a carrier are necessities for any cat. The following items may be considered luxuries, although many cats (and owners) can't live without them.

Scratching Post

Cats have to scratch; it's an instinctual behavior that cannot be curbed. Even cats that have been declawed go through the motions of scratching. If you want to protect your favorite furniture, drapes, rugs, and other items from being ripped to shreds by your new pet, you need to provide a suitable scratching post.

A scratching post helps to keep your cat from destroying your sofa or ripping your drapes.

If you own multiple cats, consider buying a "kitty condo," which allows your cats to climb, jump, and hide.

There are a wide variety of scratching objects on the market. The traditional scratching post is typically covered with carpet or a rope material called sisal, which cats find irresistible. Some also have toys attached to them to draw your cat's attention. Costs vary depending on what the post is made of, how big it is, and where you buy it. However, if you're handy with tools, you can easily make your own scratching post with a few pieces of wood and a carpet remnant.

A natural alternative to the traditional scratching post is the disposable scratching box made of thick corrugated cardboard. These products lie flat on the floor or are hung from a door handle, and cats really enjoy them. Some brands even come with a small packet of catnip to entice your kitty to use them. Our cat, Rhianna, loves her cardboard scratching boxes so much that she goes through about one a month. Luckily, they don't cost very much at all.

If you have the money and the room, you might want to invest in a so-called "kitty condo"—a structure made of wood and carpet that contains cubbyholes and high perches from which your cat can watch the world. These structures, which can be found in most pet retail outlets, combine all of your cat's favorite activities—scratching, climbing, jumping, hiding, and napping—and are especially useful in multi-cat households. The price of a kitty condo may be high, depending on complexity and materials. But again, if you're handy with tools, you can probably make your own.

Whatever scratching toy you buy, make sure that it is stable and won't topple over the first time your cat uses it. If your pet is frightened by a falling scratching post, chances are good she will never go near it again. It's also important that you place the post in an area where the cat spends a lot of time, such as in the living room, family room, or bedroom. If your new pet seems to enjoy sharpening her claws on a particular piece of furniture, place the scratching post nearby so she will have a ready alternative. (A pinch or two of catnip on the material will draw her attention.) Make sure you praise your pet every time she uses the post. If you have more than one cat, or if your cat has been sharpening her claws on furniture throughout the house, consider buying (or building) multiple posts.

Toys

Contrary to popular belief, cats do not spend their entire day napping. They are inquisitive, energetic animals (well, most of them) that love nothing more than playing with toys. Not only is play good exercise for your pet, but it also provides an opportunity for the two of you to bond together more closely.

Pet retail stores are chock-full of cat toys, from the very plain (a simple toy mouse) to the complex (a plastic ring with a ball inside that cats can knock around with their paws). But before going hog-wild, take a moment to evaluate your cat's personality. Is she gregarious or timid? Rambunctious or staid? Energetic or fat and lazy? These are important considerations, because cats are very particular about the toys they enjoy, and getting the wrong toy will be a waste of your money and your cat's time. A gregarious, energetic cat would probably enjoy a plastic ball with a noisemaker inside, whereas a shy cat might be intimidated by it. Beware of toys that are too big for your pet, because she'll probably just ignore them.

There are, however, some toys that seem to have universal appeal. A small feather on a string is something almost all cats enjoy chasing around. Soft, fuzzy play balls (perhaps scented with catnip) are also very popular. And many cat owners report hours of fun letting their pets chase the red dot from an electronic laser

Toys of all kinds are very important to your cat's health and happiness.

pointer. Of course, you don't have to spend a lot of money on playthings for your pet. Rhianna enjoys nothing more than playing "kitty hockey" around the house with a wadded-up piece of paper or a jellybean. With toys, start small and cheap and work your way up, but make sure your cat has at least a couple of toys to call her own.

Beds

Cats sleep where they want to sleep, preferably somewhere that's quiet, warm, and comfortable, like your bed or favorite chair. Many will sleep in a special cat bed, but this is something that can't be forced.

If you think your pet might enjoy her own pillow or cushion, it's probably wise to buy one that's relatively inexpensive, just in case your kitty ultimately isn't interested. Cat beds, which typically are little more than padded cushions with a frame and possibly a top, range in cost depending on brand, style, and materials. You can encourage your cat to use her new bed by placing something she likes to sleep on, such as one of your old shirts or a towel, on the cushion. This will attract your cat with a familiar scent.

Location is also important. Remember the key words—quiet, warm, and comfortable. This means away from main traffic areas, small children, and other pets such as dogs. During the winter months, you may find your cat more willing to use her own bed if you place it near a fireplace or heating vent. Cats are

Pet stores sell lots of toys, ranging from the plain mouse to complex toys like this one. Homemade toys can be fun, too.

THE GUIDE TO OWNING A CAT

If you buy your cat a comfy cat bed or cushion, make sure she'll use it by placing it in a location where she often sleeps.

creatures of comfort and naturally seek out a warm environment.

CAT-PROOFING YOUR HOME

One of the most important things you must do before bringing your new cat home for the first time is to eliminate all potential hazards, a process known as cat-proofing. As noted earlier, cats are curious creatures, and your new pet will immediately investigate every nook, cranny, corner, and cubbyhole in your house. In doing so, she may come across household items that you never think twice about but which may be hazardous to your cat's health. The following is a list of items to watch out for.

Household Chemicals

Most chemicals have a foul smell that will keep your cat at bay, but many do not,

You never know where your new kitty will end up when she explores. Remove all potentially harmful items from your cat's reach before you bring her home.

Shiny holiday bows and tinsel, balloons, ribbons, and strings of all kinds are choking hazards. Be extra careful to keep these items away from your cat.

so it's important that all household cleaning agents, paint, paint remover, fertilizer, pesticides, antifreeze, motor oil, gasoline, and other compounds be stored in pet-proof containers. Think of your pet as a curious toddler and view your house accordingly. Is there anything that could poison or otherwise injure your pet? Don't assume that chemicals are beyond your cat's reach simply because they're stored in cupboards. Many cats are very adept at opening cupboards and checking out whatever is inside. If your cat has this talent, you might want to invest in some inexpensive cupboard locks, which are available at most hardware stores and baby boutiques.

Choking Objects

Cats love to chew on and play with string, ribbon, Christmas tinsel, deflated balloons, and similar objects. Unfortunately, all of these are choking hazards and should be kept away from your pet. Birthdays and holidays are especially hazardous times, so extra caution should be exercised when your family is opening presents and disposing of string and ribbon. If even a small piece is left lying anywhere in your house, your cat will almost certainly find it. When I was a child, our cat Mokie began choking on a small deflated balloon that had been overlooked when we cleaned up after a family birthday party. Luckily, my father had the presence of mind to pull the balloon out of Mokie's throat, saving her life. We learned a valuable lesson from that frightening experience!

Electrical Hazards

There's a scene in the movie *National Lampoon's Christmas Vacation* in which the Griswold's family cat is electrocuted while chewing on some Christmas lights. The over-the-top scene is played for laughs, but it points out a very serious concern—electrical hazards. Dissuade your cat from playing with or chewing on electrical cords, and make sure all extension and appliance cords are in good condition, not frayed or broken. Exposed electrical sockets should also be covered, just to be on the safe side.

Hidden Spaces

Cats love small, dark places in which they can curl up and take a nap. Some places, such as linen closets, make a great refuge for cats in need of a little peace and quiet, and there's nothing wrong with letting your cat take advantage of them. But others, such as basements, attics, crawl spaces, garages, storage containers, small holes in wallboard, and kitchen cupboards are potentially hazardous and should always be closed to your pet. As a rule of thumb, a hiding place for your cat should be completely free of potential danger and easy for you to access. There's nothing more difficult than trying to remove a cat from a space only she can get to.

It's also a good idea to double-check clothes dryers and other appliances before turning them on. A frightening number of cats are injured or killed each year when they crawl into clothes dryers for a quick nap. Their owners then turn the machines on, not knowing their pets are inside. The same caution goes for old refrigerators, storage cabinets, and other containers that a curious cat might find of interest. Always know where your pet is before leaving the house for an extended period. Kittens should be kept in a safe room or comfortable holding pen until they're old enough for you to trust.

INDOORS ONLY?

The common wisdom used to be that cats were happiest when they were allowed to roam outdoors. They got lots of exercise and were able to engage in typical feline behavior, such as hunting and climbing. However, that belief is no longer valid. Almost all veterinary experts now believe that cats should be kept indoors at all times. By doing so, you are protecting your cat's health, increasing her lifespan, and protecting indigenous wildlife such as songbirds, small mammals, and reptiles.

Life in the wild is not easy, even for cats that have a home to return to in the evening, say veterinarians and animal-control officials. Studies have shown that

If your cat craves the outdoors but you wish to keep her safely indoors, leash-training may be an excellent compromise for both of you.

Another option for an indoor cat is a specially constructed enclosure designed to let the cat safely experience the outdoors.

the average lifespan for a stray or outdoor cat is around three years, whereas an indoor cat can live well into her teens and longer. If you keep your cat indoors all the time, she can be a part of your life for a much longer period of time.

The lifespan of an outdoor cat is short because the hazards are many, notes Wayne Hunthausen, DVM, owner of Animal Behavior Consultations in Westwood, Kansas. "The risk of getting hit by a car is high, as is the risk of being attacked by predators such as dogs," Hunthausen warns. "Outdoor cats also face exposure to life-threatening diseases such as rabies, feline leukemia, and the FIV virus."

Identification

However, even indoor cats manage to escape sometimes, which is why it's important that your cat wear some sort of identification at all times. The most common method of feline identification

is the safety collar and tag, but a wide variety of alternatives have become available in recent years, including tattoos, implantable microchips, and tiny ear tags. If you acquired your cat from a shelter or animal-control facility, she may already have one of these forms of identification. If not, discuss the issue with your veterinarian. Cats seldom give advance notice when they're going to make a run for it, and an indoor cat is especially vulnerable if trapped outdoors. Identification greatly enhances the chances of a safe and speedy return.

Indeed, identification can mean the difference between life and death for your pet if she does escape. According to Jack Sparks, director of communications for the American Humane Association, a recent study concluded that only 2 out of every 100 unidentified cats brought to shelters are returned to their owners. A small percentage of the rest are adopted out, and those that aren't face life behind bars (if they're lucky enough to be brought to a no-kill facility) or euthanasia.

Keeping an Indoor Cat Occupied

Keeping a cat indoors after she has had a taste of the great wide open can be a challenge, but it is one that you absolutely must meet. Some cats will hunker near doorways, waiting for someone to unwittingly let them out. Others will howl in protest, angry at being kept inside. Make sure all family members, friends, and neighbors are aware that your cat is not to go outside at any time, and that they should always close the door behind them. If necessary, post a small sign on your door notifying guests that your cat is never to be let outside.

You can make things easier for your pet by making sure she has plenty to do

A collar and identification tag is the best way to keep your cat safe in case of an escape.

Give your cat plenty of playtime, love, and attention, and her indoor-only life can be both safe and completely satisfying.

indoors. Give her toys to play with as well as a lot of affectionate attention. In other words, give her a reason to want to stay inside! After a while, your cat will settle in, and her need to be outdoors will subside. (If it's a male cat, having him neutered will also help calm his need to wander.) Remember: A screened window with a wide sill gives your pet the opportunity to view the world without ever stepping outside. Just make sure both the window and screen are secure and that your cat can't push them open.

One final tip: Take a good color photograph of your cat at the earliest opportunity. In the event that your cat does escape, a picture of the animal on flyers can dramatically increase her chances of recovery. If your cat is a kitten, make sure you update your photos every couple of months.

Behavior and Training

One of the most challenging aspects of cat ownership—especially for first-time cat owners—is understanding a cat's

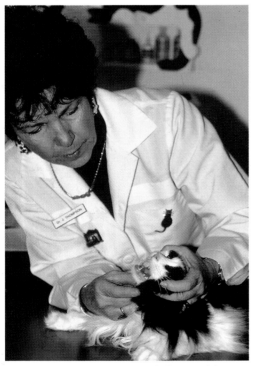

A change in your cat's regular habits could mean that she is ill. Take her to the vet at the first sign of strange behavior.

personality and behaviors. While some cats are perfect little angels, the majority will misbehave on occasion no matter how good you are to them. It's not that they're being intentionally bad, it's just their nature, and bad behaviors are very often the result of instinctual behaviors that are beyond their—and our—control.

The personalities of cats are as distinctive as our own. Just like people, no two cats are exactly alike—each is unique in a wide variety of ways. Some are friendly and personable, and others are standoffish. Some are energetic and full of fun, while others make it abundantly clear that they prefer to spend their days in quiet repose. If you get your cat when she is relatively young, you will also notice how her personality changes according to her age and surroundings.

What should you expect in a normal feline personality? Just that your cat will behave like a cat! A healthy, well-adjusted

Although they may look alike, no two cats are exactly the same.

Most misbehaving cats won't respond to loud yelling, and hitting is a definite no-no.

cat craves attention and enjoys company, likes to play (on her own terms), sleeps a lot (catnaps rather than a deep slumber), is energetic when awake, eats and uses her litter box on a fairly regular daily schedule,

A healthy, well-adjusted cat will not lash out except to defend herself. Make sure young children play with the cat gently to prevent an aggressive outburst.

and grooms herself thoroughly and often. A change in any of these characteristics could indicate that your pet is ill and should be seen by a veterinarian.

It's important that you understand that cats are creatures of habit. Unlike dogs, which go with the flow, cats usually have a set routine and don't like changes in their lives. Sudden, unexpected changes, such as the arrival of a baby or a move to another house, can affect a cat in such a way that she begins to behave inappropriately, perhaps urinating outside of her litter box or acting in an aggressive manner. Some people try to correct their misbehaving kitties with a swat of the hand or other physical punishment. Don't do this! A cat should never be hit or struck in anger or as punishment. Physical violence against a cat will not change her behavior. It will only make the animal fear you, which could lead to even more behavior problems. There are far better solutions than hitting and screaming.

The following are some of the most common feline behavior issues and how to correct them.

AGGRESSION

Cats express aggression in a number of ways (biting, scratching, and hissing) and for a variety of reasons, the most common being a perceived invasion of their established territory, such as by another cat, a dog, or a small child. Cats will also express aggressive tendencies if they are threatened, frightened, or ill.

A healthy, well-adjusted cat will not lash out unless extremely provoked. This could occur if someone accidentally steps on the cat's tail or a toddler plays with her a little too hard, and in most instances the event is over almost as quickly as it starts.

The solution to this form of aggression is easy: Be nicer to your pet, watch where you're walking, and make sure family members play with her more gently.

Other forms of aggression include the following:

Play Aggression

Play aggression is a common problem, especially among cats that were not properly disciplined as kittens. Play aggression is usually characterized by playful attacks on your feet or hands that involve teeth and claws. Your cat doesn't mean to hurt you. She's just playing, although much too roughly. This problem can be prevented by making sure that kittens know that hands and feet are not acceptable playthings, and it can be avoided by giving your cat a suitable play substitute, such as a toy mouse or a play ball. Play aggression should be countered

Encouraging your cat to attack stuffed toys in place of your hands and ankles will go a long way toward preventing play aggression.

with a sharp "No!" but never physical violence. Slapping or hitting a cat that is "playing" with your feet or hands will only make her more aggressive.

Overstimulation

This form of aggression is commonly seen in kittens that are played with too much, but it's also an all-too-frequent indicator that your cat has had enough petting, scratching, or whatever else you're doing to her at the moment. Most overstimulated cats will give you a light smack with their paws or a gentle but insistent bite to let you know that they're ready to stop—and you'd better listen, because to continue the activity is to risk serious injury. If your cat suddenly becomes enraged and really starts to bite or scratch, don't attempt to fight back. That will only make the situation worse. Instead, yell sharply or slap your palm on a table or wall to startle the animal. At that point, it will probably run away. To prevent a repeat, learn to read your cat's personality cues and act accordingly.

Redirected Aggression

This problem typically occurs when your cat has become agitated by something she cannot control, such as a strange cat in her yard. Instead of attacking the intruder, your cat lashes out at you. There's not much you can do about this problem, aside from ensuring that strange cats and other animals cannot enter your property and blocking your cat's view of the outdoors.

Pain

Cats are very reluctant to express pain. This goes back to the days when cats lived in the wild, where any sign of illness or injury made them an easy target for larger predators. As a result, it's sometimes difficult to determine if a cat is ill—but sudden, unprovoked aggression can be one clue, especially if the cat reacts violently if you simply touch her or try to hold her. In cases such as this, it's best to let your cat calm down, then gently place her in a carrier and take her to your veterinarian for an examination.

Similarly, fear can also make a cat aggressive. Loud noises, unfamiliar scents, strange people, large animals—all of these can frighten a cat and cause her to lash out violently. If this occurs, remove the cause of the cat's fear and let her calm down on her own. Most of the time, a frightened cat will seek out a quiet refuge, such as under the bed or in a closet, and stay there until she feels safe.

DESTRUCTIVE BEHAVIOR

Destructive feline behavior usually falls into two categories—scratching and chewing. In order to correct this problem, it's important that you understand why your kitty is behaving this way.

Scratching

Scratching, or "claw-sharpening," is an instinctual behavior over which cats have no control. As noted earlier, even cats that have been declawed still go through the motions of sharpening their claws.

Cats scratch for a variety of reasons. It doesn't really sharpen their claws, but it does help remove old claw sheaths (which you'll occasionally find embedded in your

Scratching helps a cat remove her old claw sheaths, revealing the sharper claw beneath.

rug and elsewhere), revealing the sharper layer underneath. It is also a form of stretching that cats inherently enjoy. Scratching is also a marking behavior—the pads on a cat's feet secrete a special scent, leaving a message behind on anything the cat runs her claws over. Unfortunately, this enjoyable activity often comes at the expense of your furniture, drapes, and rugs! This is usually because you have provided no alternatives, such as a scratching post. In most cases, that's the best way to stop destructive scratching behavior.

If your cat continues to claw the furniture occasionally even after you've given her a scratching post, it's time to take the battle to another level. One answer is to cover the cat's favorite scratching surfaces with aluminum foil. Cats dislike the texture and shine of aluminum foil and will avoid it whenever possible. After a week or so of redirecting your cat away from that spot and onto her scratching post (adding a few pinches of catnip to entice her if necessary), you should be able to remove the aluminum foil without having to worry.

Another option is to squirt your cat with a water gun or mist bottle every time she starts to claw anything but her scratching post. A little water won't hurt your cat, but it will certainly give her something to think about. For best results, spray your cat so that it appears as if the water came out of nowhere. After a while, she'll get the message, and she won't associate you with the spritzing.

One thing you need to remember is that your cat isn't scratching up your house out of anger or spite. These are human characteristics that don't really apply to cats, no matter how things may appear.

Keeping your cat's claws clipped will help prevent damage to your furniture from scratching.

Squirting your cat with a water gun or startling her with a loud noise can help keep your plant-loving cat from misbehaving.

Cats react and behave instinctually, and scratching is part of that. So don't think your cat has it in for you! She doesn't—she is just behaving normally.

Chewing

Chewing is another common form of destructive feline behavior. It feels good to the cat, and it also leaves scent messages on the object in question. Common "victims" of chewing include clothing, books, and plants. The best way to correct this behavior is to remove the object or make it as unattractive as possible. For example, if your cat enjoys chewing on your favorite sweater, keep the sweater in a drawer or covered box and give your cat a substitute item to chew on, such as a sheepskin-covered toy.

Plants often suffer great damage at the hands—or teeth—of cats. Not only is this aggravating to you, but it's potentially dangerous to your pet if the plant in question is poisonous. (To determine if any plants in your home are hazardous to your pets, consult your veterinarian or your local poison control center.)

Cats can be dissuaded from chewing on plants by placing foil or pebbles in and around the pot, applying a foul-tasting substance such as hot sauce to the plant's leaves, or hanging all of your indoor plants from the ceiling (a last-ditch solution, to be sure). And don't forget your trusty squirt gun. Every time your cat starts to wander too close to your houseplants, give her a good squirt. After a couple of unexpected hits, she'll never go near another plant again!

VOCALIZATION

Vocalization, or loud, incessant meowing, isn't really a destructive behavior, but it can be extremely irritating to everyone in the household. Some breeds, such as Siamese, are more prone to talkativeness than others, but many cats vocalize because they have been inadvertently trained to do so by over-accommodating owners.

Do you leap up and attend to your cat every time she lets out a meow? If so, you're just as guilty as your pet, because you've demonstrated that all she has to do is make noise to get her way. My wife and I were guilty of this ourselves. Our cat Rhianna learned early on that if she wanted scratches in the morning, all she had to do was jump up on our bed and start meowing. We foolishly gave in to this behavior at the beginning and soon found our mornings starting at 5 a.m.! We finally broke her of this habit by ignoring her. She meowed a lot at first but eventually got the message and no longer bothers us until we get up.

You can combat excessive vocalization the same way. Don't cater to your cat's every whim. Set patterns and schedules for feeding, grooming, scratching, playing, and so forth, and stick to them no matter how raucous your cat becomes. After a while, she will come to understand that meowing won't make you jump, and the vocalization will cease.

GARBAGE-RAIDING

You can't really blame your cat for tipping over the garbage can if you've left half a chicken in there. It's only natural for your kitty to want a taste of something that smells so delicious. Unfortunately, garbage-raiding can result in a horrible mess as well as pose a danger to your pet by exposing her to hazardous chemicals and dangerous leftovers such as chicken and turkey bones, which can easily splinter and pierce an animal's trachea if they are swallowed.

The best way to prevent garbage-raiding is to make sure that all trash and garbage cans in your house have tight lids or are located in areas that are inaccessible to your pet, such as a pantry or laundry room. It's that simple.

LITTER PROBLEMS

There are few things more aggravating than a cat that refuses to use her litter box. This is one of the most common problems faced by cat owners and is one of the primary reasons that cats are abandoned at shelters.

There are a number of reasons why a cat may refuse to use her litter box. When all else fails, consult your vet.

Multiple-cat households may benefit from having multiple litter boxes. One box per cat should be adequate.

Cats refuse to use their litter boxes for a wide variety of reasons. Yours may not have been properly litter-trained as a kitten. She may be a finicky animal that urinates or defecates outside her box because the litter isn't clean enough. She may not like the location of the box, the type of litter she is forced to use, or the fact that she must share her box with other cats. She may have been frightened while using the box and no longer wish to go there. Or, she may be ill.

Fixing a litter box problem may require some trial and error, because your pet can't come out and tell you exactly why she's behaving the way she is. If your cat has always used her litter box properly, then suddenly stops for no apparent reason, your first consideration should be illness. I speak from experience on this.

Rhianna had always been good about using her litter box, even after we moved a long distance. Then one day, she started urinating on the living room carpet. We noticed that her urine appeared to be darker than usual, and we took her to the vet for a checkup. The diagnosis: A urinary tract infection. After two weeks of antibiotics, she was as good as new and back to her usual fastidious habits.

A sick cat may accidentally urinate out of the box and then go back to that spot because of the odor. Once the cat's illness has been cured and the spot sufficiently cleaned (diluted white vinegar works quite well), you shouldn't have any more problems.

The following are a few handy tips for correcting litter box problems that are not associated with illness:

- Consider the location of your cat's litter box. If it's in a high-traffic area, your cat may not feel comfortable using it because she has no privacy. Move the box to a place that is more quiet, such as a seldom-used bathroom, closet, or pantry. A cover on the box will provide even more privacy and security.
- Clean your cat's litter at least once a day, and even more often if she's finicky. Cats have a sensitive sense of smell and are put off by harsh odors. A litter box that is not cleaned on a regular basis can start to smell, and your cat will notice it before you do.
- Be wary of changing to a different type of litter. While most cats couldn't care less about the type of litter you use, some care a lot and will demonstrate their disapproval by urinating or defecating elsewhere. If your cat is happy with a particular brand, stick with it.
- Consider multiple litter boxes for multiple cats. Some cats are very territorial and don't take kindly to sharing their box with another. In addition, multiple cats using a single box means more frequent cleaning. If you neglect the box for even a day, things can get stinky and send your pets fleeing.
- Make sure you immediately clean the area your cat has soiled to eliminate the odor and prevent your cat from returning there. If necessary, lay down a couple of sheets of aluminum foil to keep your cat at bay.
- As a last-ditch effort, confine your cat to a crate or pen with her bed and a

Indoor spraying is often a sign of anxiety or fear and can occur in both male and female cats.

The introduction of other animals or people to a household can cause an outbreak of spraying. Make sure to handle any introductions slowly and carefully.

litter box. Cats are reluctant to soil where they sleep, so your cat will have to use the litter box. Your goal is to retrain the cat to use the litter box to relieve herself. Let the cat out when you can watch her, but place her in the pen right away if you notice her starting to look for a place to go to the bathroom. If an accident occurs, wipe it up with a napkin and place the napkin in the litter box so your cat learns to make the association. Once the proper habit is reestablished, gradually shift the litter box to its previous location.

One last word on this issue: Don't punish your cat for not using her litter box, because she simply won't understand why you're angry. Yelling at your cat, hitting her, or rubbing her face in her mess will not solve the problem. It will only make your cat afraid of you and more secretive about her litter box behavior.

SPRAYING

Indoor spraying is quite different from traditional litter box avoidance but just as aggravating. This problem is most commonly associated with unneutered male cats, but it can occur with all cats—male or female, fixed or unfixed.

Spraying is a marking behavior, not a litter box issue. Cats spray to let other cats know that they've been there and to identify a territory as their own. It is usually performed standing up (unlike urination, which is typically done in a squatting position) and involves a small amount of urine being squirted backward on vertical surfaces such as furniture and walls. The smell of marking spray is also typically more noticeable than plain urine.

Cats often start spraying because of changes in their environment or lives, such as a move to a new house or the introduction of other animals or people into the family. A cat that has trouble adapting to the change, or one that feels fearful or anxious, may indicate her fretfulness by spraying. In other words, the cat is under pressure, and spraying is one way that she tries to make herself feel better. The pungent scent of the spray is one the animal readily recognizes, and she finds this comforting.

Correcting indoor spraying can be a challenge. One of the simplest solutions is to have the animal fixed, if this hasn't been done already. Cats that have been spayed or neutered are generally much more calm, which greatly diminishes their need to spray.

It's also important that you identify the source of your cat's anxiety and do what you can to make the cat feel better. If you've just brought home a new baby, for example, you may find that you haven't been paying as much attention to your cat as you used to. The cat may sense your changed priority and deal with it by spraying. Many times, a cat will stop spraying once she comes to terms with the source of her anxiety, such as a long-distance move, but not always.

As with litter box avoidance, it is important that you clean a sprayed spot immediately so that the cat will not return and spray the area again. One effective cleaning method is to wash the soiled area with a mixture of water and baking soda, then scrub it with pure alcohol or even vodka. Make sure you swab a small piece of hidden material first to make sure it won't run or fade. Let the area dry naturally, or dry it with a hair dryer. Keep the cat from returning for a few days by covering the area with aluminum foil or some other material that your cat doesn't like. The smell should fade after a short while, and your pet will be less inclined to respray there.

Remember, cats are comforted by familiar scents. When you do your spring or winter cleaning, you are eliminating many of the natural scents that make your cat feel relaxed and welcome. Always leave a little something that your cat will recognize as her own, such as a favorite towel or bedspread. If you completely eliminate all scents, your cat may become anxious and start to spray. Similarly, if you move into a new house, it may be a good idea to keep your cat confined until the old scents of your furniture and belongings mingle with the unfamiliar scents of your new house. After a while, your cat will accept the place as her home.

If your cat continues to spray no matter what you do, consult your veterinarian or an animal behaviorist for further advice. There are products on the market designed to eliminate spray odors and prevent cats from further marking, but you should discuss them with your vet before using them.

Your Cat's Health

Cats are not difficult animals to care for. If she is kept indoors, treated well, fed well, and regularly checked by a veterinarian, the average cat will live well into her teens and sometimes longer.

The care of your cat is actually a partnership between you and your veterinarian. By working together, you can ensure that your cat remains healthy and that any medical concerns are addressed promptly.

Your new cat should be examined by a veterinarian within a day or so of being brought home, and always before being introduced to other cats in your family. Regardless of where you acquired your pet, she should be given a thorough examination for signs of parasites, inherited diseases, and other potential problems. If she's old enough, she should receive vaccinations for rabies, feline leukemia, FIV, and other common communicable disorders. Vaccination protocols differ greatly from region to region, so consult your veterinarian for the schedule in your area.

As your cat ages, her need for regular veterinary checkups increases. The older a cat gets, the more prone she is to certain health problems, and it's important that you and your vet stay on top of things. Thankfully, most health problems experienced by cats are treatable if detected early.

SIGNS OF ILLNESS

You can ensure your cat's good health by checking her regularly for early signs of illness. The areas to examine include:

Eyes

The eyes should be wide open and free of inflammation or discharge.

Ears

Watch out for redness, inflammation, or an abnormal smell or waxy discharge. All of these can be signs of an ear infection or other problem. The presence of tiny

Your veterinarian should be contacted whenever your cat is sick. By working together with your vet, you can help your cat live a long, healthy life.

specks similar to coffee grounds could indicate mites.

Mouth

Examine your cat for sore, red gums; open lesions; or extremely bad breath (a sign of gum disease, among other illnesses). And every now and then, watch your cat when she eats. Does she appear to experience discomfort? If so, have her checked by a vet right away.

Nose

A runny nasal discharge could indicate a cold or upper respiratory infection. However, slight dampness without a discharge is normal.

Coat

Cats are fastidious groomers and usually take very good care of their skin and coats. Fur that is dull, patchy, or matted could indicate parasites or other problems. A cat

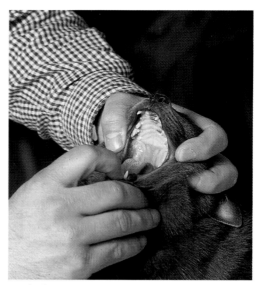

Don't forget to examine your cat's mouth for sore, red gums, open lesions, or bad breath, all of which may be signs of dental disease.

that grooms herself incessantly, to the point where she chews away her fur, could be suffering from skin allergies.

Anus

Cats don't particularly like it when you go poking around "back there." It's no fun for the owner either, but it is important that you examine your cat's anus on a regular basis. Signs of rectal bleeding should be reported to a veterinarian. Tiny specks on or around the anus could indicate the presence of intestinal parasites.

ZOONOTIC DISEASES

While many contagious diseases contracted by cats are species-specific, some, which are called zoonotic diseases, can be transferred to humans. It's always wise to be careful when handling a cat that is obviously ill. But precautions should be taken even when handling a healthy cat,

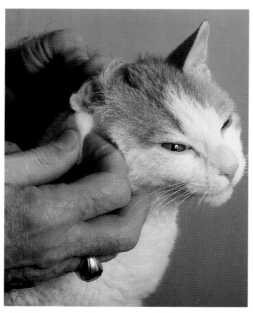

Check your cat's ears regularly for redness, inflammation, an abnormal smell, or waxy discharge. Tiny brown specks may be a sign of ear mites.

Lethargy or a lack of interest in her usual daily activities may be a sign that your cat is sick. Have her examined by a veterinarian as soon as possible.

especially if your own health is compromised in some way. Pregnant women, for example, should be very careful not to touch cat feces because of the risk of contracting toxoplasmosis, a disease caused by the protozoan parasite *Toxoplasma gondii*. The disease poses little risk to healthy adults but can cause death or miscarriage if contracted by a fetus through the placenta. Because of this very serious danger, pregnant women are advised not to clean a cat's litter box. If they absolutely must do so, they should wear thick plastic gloves and a mask and dispose of the feces in a closed plastic bag.

SPAYING AND NEUTERING

Should you have your cat spayed or neutered? The answer to this question is easy—yes! Unless you plan to breed or show your cat, there is no reason at all not to have her fixed. Not only does it benefit your cat's health, but it goes a long way toward reducing the population of unwanted cats in this country.

The reasons people give for not having their cats spayed or neutered are many, but none of them hold up on close analysis. They include:

- "I want my cat to enjoy motherhood." Why? Bearing kittens is no picnic for the mother, and then *you're* stuck finding homes for all the little ones.
- "I want my children to witness the joy of birth." If that's the case, buy your children a book or video and get your cat fixed. Why should your pet have to be a living medical museum?

Yes, kittens are cute, but that's no excuse for letting your beloved pet breed at random. Keep your cat healthier and more content—and help reduce pet overpopulation—by having him or her neutered or spayed.

• "I could never have my male cat fixed— it's just not natural!" Veterinarians hear this a lot from men, and it's absolute nonsense. Cats don't have to mate, and those who never have done so don't miss it in the least. The medical procedure for neutering male cats is quick and simple. Most cats can go home the same day, with no side effects at all. Animals that have been fixed are more docile, less inclined to roam, and less likely to engage in destructive behavior such as spraying. They will experience better health over the course of their lives. If you don't want to be fixed yourself, that's fine. But you're doing your pet a great injustice by letting him breed indiscriminately.

According to veterinarians, the ideal time to have a female cat spayed is around five months of age, shortly before she goes into heat for the first time. However, the operation can take place anytime after that, with the only provision being that the cat is not in heat or nursing. Male cats should be neutered at around six months of age.

SHOULD YOU DECLAW?

Declawing is an issue about which there is strong debate within the cat-care community. Some people see nothing wrong with it, while others believe it is an unnecessary form of mutilation. Even many veterinarians feel this way and strongly discourage their clients who wish to have their cats declawed.

Most owners have their cats declawed because their pets have started ripping up the furniture, and declawing the cats is far easier than taking the time to retrain them. It's an issue that can be decided only by you and your veterinarian, but make sure to give it a lot of thought. Declawing is a relatively simple surgical procedure, but the healing process can be lengthy and very painful. Also, if it isn't done properly, the claws can grow back, requiring yet more surgery.

If your decision to have your cat declawed is based on destructive behavior, try some of the tips offered in this book before bringing your cat in for surgery. Most cats can be easily trained to use a scratching post, saving you both a lot of aggravation.

THE AGING CAT

Older cats, like older people, sometimes need a little more care and attention than those that are younger. Indeed, the signs of old age in cats are very similar to those in humans. Older cats tend to be less active and sleep more, lose or gain weight, and experience age-related health problems such as arthritis. According to veterinarians, a 10-year-old cat is the equivalent of a 56-year-old person. At age 22, a cat is the human equivalent of 100 years of age.

Regular visits to your veterinarian will help keep your aging cat in relatively good health. You can also help by making sure your cat is comfortable, safe, and happy. This means protecting her from other animals, making sure she is warm and cozy in inclement weather, and making small adjustments such as placing a stool next

Overgrown nails can be a problem for the elderly cat. Gently clipping your cat's claws is a good idea.

to her favorite windowsill when age makes jumping more difficult.

Older cats need just as much attention, if not more, than younger cats. That's because they just aren't as energetic as they once were, and playing doesn't hold the appeal it once did. Aging cats also tend to feel more vulnerable and thus demand more of their owners' time. Sometimes this manifests itself in a phenomenon known as "night calling," in which a cat starts meowing plaintively after everyone has gone to bed. Once her owner reappears and gives her a gentle pet, the animal is reassured and usually goes off to sleep.

If your elderly pet is a long-haired cat, she may need a little extra grooming to keep mats from forming. It's also a good idea to keep an eye on your cat's claws as she grows older. Elderly cats are more prone to overgrown nails, and the more

Believe it or not, that feisty little kitten will one day become a feline senior citizen. The signs of old age in cats are very similar to those in humans.

THE GUIDE TO OWNING A CAT

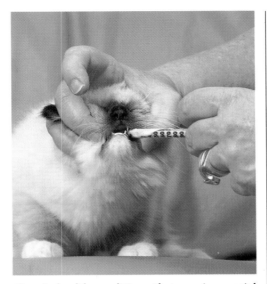

Chronic health conditions that require special medical care at home, such as syringe feeding or insulin shots, may develop as your cat ages.

brittle claws of an older cat may not retract as well as they once did. As a result, their claws can become caught on carpets, causing injury and pain. If your cat's claws become too long, gently clip them. If your cat simply won't tolerate this, ask your veterinarian to do it.

Older cats may develop chronic health conditions such as diabetes or kidney problems. Many of these ailments can be treated effectively, allowing an older cat to live out her final years in relative comfort. But when they can't, you will have to say goodbye. Having a cat put to sleep is never easy, but usually it's the best thing for all concerned. When making this decision, ask yourself about the quality of life your cat would have if you let the illness go on. No one wants a beloved pet to suffer. Rest assured that euthanasia is quick and painless. Your veterinarian can give you the specifics when the time comes.

PARASITES

Parasites are probably the most common complaint seen by veterinarians, especially among cats that are allowed to roam outdoors. Free-range cats often come in contact with contaminated soil, eat contaminated rodents, and have run-ins with infected animals—another good reason to keep your pet inside at all times.

Fleas and Ticks

Without question, the most common feline parasite is fleas. Even indoor cats can get fleas, which can enter the house on their owner's clothing (as can ticks). Thankfully, with modern treatments, fleas are little more than a minor annoyance, although they can cause a

Regular grooming and the application of prescription medications can help eradicate most feline parasite problems.

serious skin reaction in cats that are allergic to them. Several very good flea products are currently available, including new liquid treatments that are placed on the back of a cat's neck. These inexpensive prescription treatments kill all the fleas on your cat within 48 hours and provide very effective control for an entire month. Other options include flea powder, shampoos, and collars. Consult your veterinarian about the best preventive treatment for your pet.

Internal Parasites

Outdoor cats, and those that come in contact with outdoor cats, are also at risk of internal parasites such as roundworms, tapeworms, and pinworms, as well as protozoal intestinal infections like coccidiosis, giardiasis, and toxoplasmosis. Most of these pests are more irritating than life-threatening, although they can

Don't let your cat eat outdoor grass, just in case it is contaminated with harmful parasite eggs.

cause serious health problems in some animals and should be treated as soon as they are detected. Symptoms of an internal or intestinal parasitic infection include small white segments in the animal's feces, weight loss, mushy diarrhea, vomiting, and poor coat. Your veterinarian can confirm parasitic infection and recommend the appropriate treatment.

The following tips can help prevent parasitic infection:

- Don't expose parasite-free pets to strange cats until the new members of the family have been given a clean bill of health by your veterinarian.
- Don't let cats roam in areas where other cats may have buried their feces.
- Don't let cats eat outdoor grass. It may look clean, but it could be contaminated with parasite eggs.
- Don't let pets eat yard-dwelling prey animals, including lizards, toads, birds, and insects. All can harbor parasites that could easily infect your pet.
- Don't let cats eat raw meat, such as chicken or pork. It may contain parasites.

FELINE VIRUSES

Cats are prone to a variety of infectious viral diseases, many of which may be prevented through regular vaccinations.

Feline Leukemia

Feline leukemia is a viral condition that compromises a cat's immune system, resulting in AIDS-like symptoms. (Don't worry—it cannot be transmitted to humans!) It also can induce anemia by attacking a cat's blood cells, resulting in

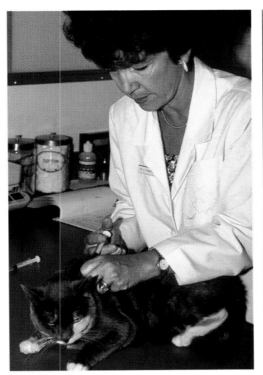
Regular vaccinations for common feline illnesses will help keep your cat healthy.

infertility and cancers of the white blood cells in the bloodstream or lymphatic tissue. The symptoms of feline leukemia depend on where in the body the cancerous growths develop, although veterinarians see a large number of problems in the lymph nodes of the chest in young cats and the intestines of older animals. A blood test can easily diagnose the condition, although there is no cure. That's why it's so important that you have your cat immunized at an early age.

Feline Immunodeficiency Virus (FIV)

This virus is similar to the human immunodeficiency virus (HIV), attacking the immune system and exposing the animal to a number of infectious conditions that it might otherwise be able to throw off. The virus is spread through saliva-to-blood contact and is commonly seen in roaming male cats that get in a lot of fights. There is no cure for this condition, nor is there presently a vaccine to prevent it. Like feline leukemia, it cannot be transmitted to humans.

Feline Infectious Peritonitis (FIP)

This life-threatening condition is caused by a virus known as a coronavirus (there are actually several coronaviruses, not all of which cause FIP) and is typically transmitted via feces and saliva. It is most commonly seen in multiple-cat households and cat breeding farms and can affect various body systems, including the brain, the digestive system, and the heart. Veterinarians are unable to cure FIP, but they can treat the localized problems that go with it, such as bacterial infections. A vaccine exists for FIP, although it usually is not necessary for cats living in single-animal households. If you're still concerned, you should discuss the issue with your veterinarian.

DIGESTIVE AND URINARY PROBLEMS

Like humans, cats may be afflicted with a wide variety of ailments of the stomach, intestines, and urinary tract. These are most common in older cats, but younger cats can get them, too, so owners should be aware of the symptoms and act accordingly.

Vomiting and Diarrhea

Vomiting and diarrhea are common symptoms of gastrointestinal disease, especially if the symptoms are chronic.

(The occasional hairball is normal and is not indicative of a gastrointestinal problem.) The most common gastrointestinal ailment in cats is inflammatory bowel disease, which is believed to be an allergic reaction to something in the cat's diet. The problem can usually be corrected by a simple change in the cat's food, but if your cat vomits several times in a 24-hour period, or if you notice blood in the vomit, take the cat to your vet immediately for a thorough examination.

Kidney Disease

This is another medical concern, especially among older cats. Causes can include infection, kidney stones, tumors, injury, poisoning, and autoimmune disease, though most cases are the result of chronic interstitial nephritis—long-term scarring brought on by years of normal wear and tear. Early symptoms of kidney disease include increased thirst, poor appetite, weight loss, and bad breath. If it is not treated promptly, kidney disease can lead to vomiting, dehydration, and death.

Kidney disease is easily diagnosed in the early stages with a blood or urine test, and it frequently can be managed with a restricted diet that is low in phosphorus.

Feline Lower Urinary Tract Disease (FLUTD)

FLUTD is also common and is usually characterized by inflammation of the cat's urinary tract. If the bladder is affected, it will cause symptoms similar to cystitis in humans. However, an accumulation of crystalline material in the lower urinary tract may also result in an obstruction to the outflow of urine from the bladder. This is especially common in male cats because their urethras are much more narrow than in females. The most common symptom is urinary straining, and the condition should be treated as an emergency. If it is not treated quickly, irreversible damage to the kidneys can result.

The causes of FLUTD are many, though the condition is most commonly seen in inactive, overweight cats. Urine that is too alkaline or too acidic may also play a role, especially in the formation of painful crystals. In cases such as these, a diet low in magnesium can help prevent a recurrence.

SKIN AILMENTS

Cats are sturdy animals, but they have very sensitive skin and are prone to a wide variety of skin conditions and ailments. External parasites such as fleas, for example, can cause an allergic reaction so severe that a cat will chew herself until her skin is raw, and fungal infections can cause unsightly bald or inflamed patches. Cats can also develop painful abscesses as a result of fights or other injury.

Because of these risks, it's important to examine your pet's entire body on a regular basis. Look closely for signs of allergic reaction, parasitic infection, or wounds, and have them attended to promptly. Most skin ailments are easily diagnosed and treated, but cats are adept at hiding

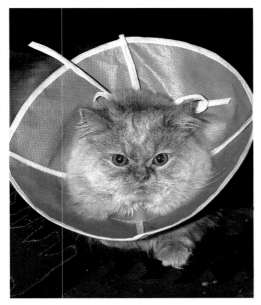

If your cat suffers from skin conditions such as severe allergies, medication and an "Elizabethan collar" may be prescribed to help her heal.

notice them. While you're examining your cat, it's also a good idea to feel her body for odd lumps and lesions. Most of the time they mean nothing, but anything out of the ordinary should be checked just to be on the safe side.

GROOMING

There's nothing a cat enjoys more than a good bath—as long as she is the one doing the bathing! Cats are extremely clean animals, and they bathe and groom themselves constantly. However, that doesn't mean that you can't lend a hand. Regular grooming sessions are a good way for you and your pet to bond with each other, and when these sessions are handled properly, both of you will greatly enjoy the experience.

health problems, and skin conditions can endure for a long time before you finally

While only a few tools and a small amount of time are required to groom most cats, long-haired breeds such as Persians need extensive daily grooming in order to look their best.

Cats are very special animals. They provide love, laughter, and affection, and don't ask for much in return. Love a cat, and you will be loved for many years to come.

You need only a couple of basic tools to groom your cat—a brush and a thin-toothed comb. Most cats love to be groomed, but shy cats may be a bit reticent at first. If your cat appears frightened or reluctant, don't push the issue. Start slowly and softly until your pet comes to realize just how good it feels. Before you know it, your kitty will be on your lap every evening demanding to be combed!

Long-haired cats, such as Persians and Himalayans, should be groomed every day, but even short-haired breeds require and enjoy a good combing now and then. Always remember to be gentle, and don't overstimulate your pet. Start at the head and neck and gradually work your way down to the tail. Don't forget the areas on the stomach and between the legs—they need attention, too. Use this opportunity to examine your pet for parasites such as fleas and ticks, as well as symptoms of other problems, including cuts, lumps, and lesions.

If you can get away with it, it's also a good idea to brush your cat's teeth on a regular basis. There are a wide variety of feline dental products on the market, including special kitty toothbrushes and toothpaste, but not all cats are keen on having their owners poke around in their mouths. If your cat doesn't mind, great. If not, have your veterinarian clean your cat's teeth at least once every couple of years. Cats are prone to gum disease, which can inhibit their ability to eat. Extremely foul breath is a common

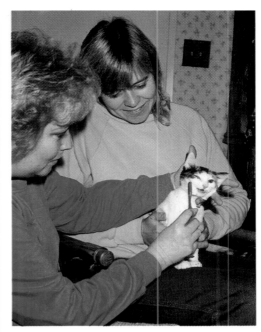

It's a good idea to brush your cat's teeth regularly. This is usually a two-person operation! If your cat won't tolerate it, have your vet clean the cat's teeth annually.

indicator of advanced dental problems.

Grooming is easiest if you start when your cat is young. Begin combing and brushing your pet while she is a kitten, and she will let you do whatever you wish for the rest of her life.

CONCLUSION

When the relationship is entered into with love and compassion, owning a cat can be a wondrous adventure. Cats are very special and unique animals, and they enrich our lives in many ways. They provide love, laughter, and affectionate company, and all they ask for in return is kindness, a full food bowl, and a warm place to curl up at night.

Love a cat, and you will be loved for many years to come.

Index

Abyssinian 13
African wild cats 3, 6
Aggression 41
Aging cat 55
American Shorthair 13
Anus 52
Beds 32
Behavior and training 38
Behavior changes 40
Best age to adopt 9
Birman 14
Breeders 16
Burmese 11
Carnivora 6
Cat carrier 29
Cat/kitten-proofing 9, 33
Children and cats 8
Coat 52
Declawing 54
Destructive behavior 42
Ears 50
Egyptians 3
Exotic Shorthair 12
Eyes 50
Felidae 6
Feline acne 26
Feline immunodeficiency virus 59
Feline infectious peritonitis 59
Feline leukemia virus 58
Feral cats 5
FLUTD 60
Food 24
Food/water bowls 26
Free kittens 17, 21
Garbage-raiding 45
Grooming 61
Health 50
Himalayan 11
History 3
Hunter-scavengers 6
Identification 36

Indoor cats 35
Kidney disease 60
Kitten vs. cat 8
Litter box 27
Litter problems 45
Litter 28
Maine Coon 12
Mouth 52
Multiple-cat households 22
Nose 52
Nutritional supplements 26
Oriental cats 11
Oriental Shorthair 13
Parasites 57
Persian 12
Pet stores 19
Price 11
Purebred vs. mixed breed 10, 12
Safety 33
Scottish Fold 13
Scratching post 29
Selecting 8
Self-domestication 5
Shelters 14
Siamese 11, 12
Skin ailments 60
Socialization, importance of 10
Spaying and neutering .53
Spraying 48
Stray cats 21
Supplies 24
Table scraps 25
Tattoo/microchip 15, 21, 36
Tonkinese 14
Toxoplasmosis 53
Toys 31
Training new cat 8
Veterinary exam 50
Vocalization 44
Vomiting/diarrhea 59
Zoonotic diseases 52

Photo Credits

Joan Balzarini, 3, 7, 10B, 22, 28, 29, 31, 33T, 38, 51, 56, 59, 61T

Richard K. Blackmon, 34

Jacquie DeLillo, 9

Isabelle Francais, 2, 10T, 11, 12-14 (all), 16, 25, 27, 33B, 39, 43B, 46, 52 (T & B), 54, 57 (T & B), 61B

Robert Pearcy, 1, 4, 5, 9T, 17, 18, 20, 30, 35, 36, 37 (T & B), 40B, 43T, 47, 48, 53, 58, 62, 63

Vince Serbin, 44

Linda Sturdy, 6, 40T, 45

John Tyson, 8, 23, 26, 32, 41, 55